NATIONAL GEOGRAPHIC
School Publishing

T0069725

Comparing Sizes and Weights

James Nguyen

PICTURE CREDITS
Illustrations by Gaston Vanzet (4–5, 14–15).
All photographs by Lindsay Edwards Photography.

Produced through the worldwide resources of the National Geographic Society, John M. Fahey, Jr., President and Chief Executive Officer; Gilbert M. Grosvenor, Chairman of the Board; Nina D. Hoffman, Executive Vice President and President, Books and Education Publishing Group.

PREPARED BY NATIONAL GEOGRAPHIC SCHOOL PUBLISHING
Ericka Markman, Senior Vice President and President Children's Books and Education Publishing Group; Steve Mico, Senior Vice President and Publisher; Marianne Hiland, Editorial Director; Lynnette Brent, Executive Editor; Michael Murphy and Barbara Wood, Senior Editors; Bea Jackson, Design Director; David Dumo, Art Director; Margaret Sidlowsky, Illustrations Director; Matt Wascavage, Manager of Publishing Services; Sean Philpotts, Production Manager.

MANUFACTURING AND QUALITY MANAGEMENT
Christopher A. Liedel, Chief Financial Officer; Phillip L. Schlosser, Director; Clifton M. Brown III, Manager.

BOOK DEVELOPMENT
Ibis for Kids Australia Pty Limited.

Copyright © 2006 National Geographic Society. All rights reserved. Reproduction of the whole or any part of the contents without written permission from the publisher is prohibited. National Geographic, National Geographic *Windows on Literacy*, and the Yellow Border are registered trademarks of the National Geographic Society.

Published by the National Geographic Society
1145 17th Street, N.W.
Washington, D.C. 20036-4688

ISBN 0-7922-6066-X

Fifth Printing 2008
Printed in China

Contents

Think and Discuss	4
Small Things	6
Tall Things	8
Long Things	10
Heavy Things	12
Use What You Learned	14
Picture Glossary	16

Pig
heavy animal
Bear
heavier animal
Elephant
heaviest animal
smallest book
smaller book
small book
long table

There are many ways to compare things.
Which things are small? Which things are long?

Small Things

Some things are small.
You can compare how small they are.

The book
is **small**.

The crayon
is **smaller** than
the book.

The penny
is the **smallest**.

Big

Big is the opposite
of small.

Tall Things

Some things are tall.
You can compare how tall they are.

The door
is the **tallest**.

Short

Short is the opposite
of tall.

Long Things

Some things are long.
You can compare how long they are.

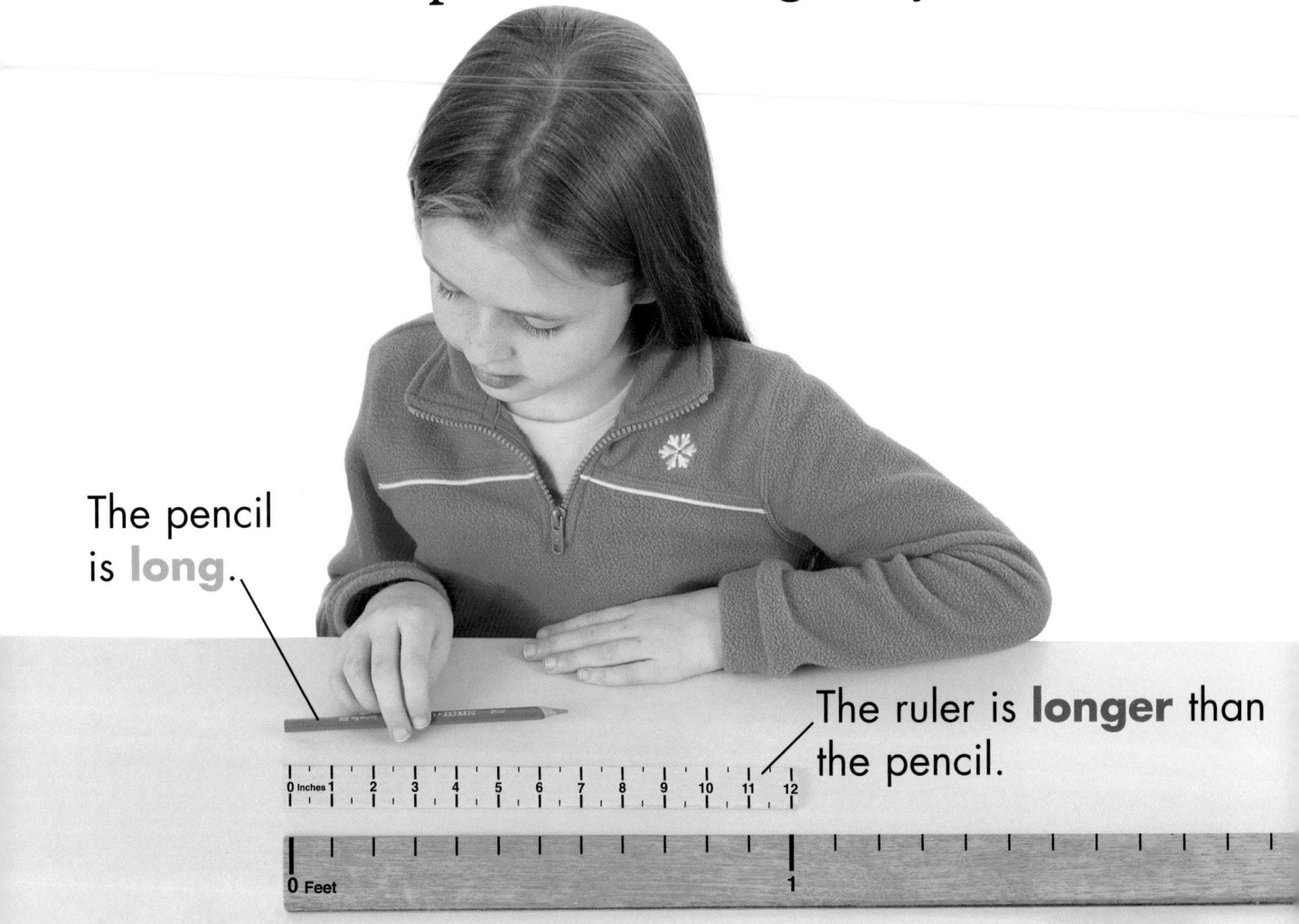

Short

Short is the opposite of long.

The yardstick is the **longest**.

Heavy Things

Some things are heavy.
You can compare how heavy they are.

The book is **heavy**.

The plant
is **heavier** than
the book.

The backpack
is the **heaviest**.

Light

Light is the opposite
of heavy.

bag
backpack
bench
ball

heavy
heavier
heaviest
long
longer
longest
small
smaller
smallest
tall
taller
tallest

Picture Glossary

small

smaller

smallest

tall

taller

tallest

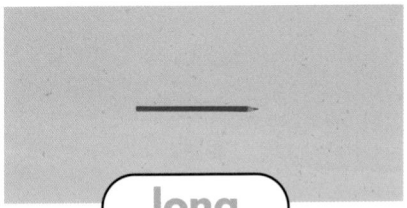

long

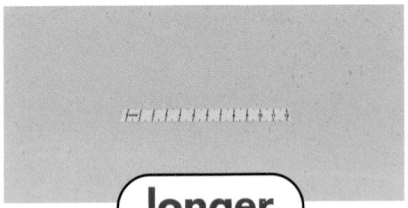

longer

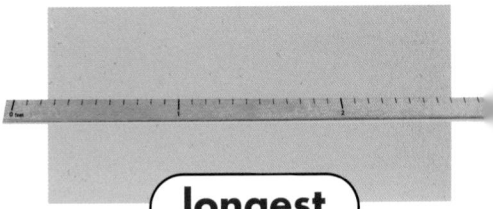

longest

heavy

heavier

heaviest